Something Beautiful for

Mother

COUNTRYMAN ®

A Division of Thomas Nelson Publishers

THOMAS NELSON ®

Since 1798

NASHVILLE DALLAS MEXICO CITY RIO DE JANEIRO

Something Beautiful for Mother

© 2012 by Thomas Nelson, Inc.

Published in Nashville, Tennessee, by Thomas Nelson®. Thomas Nelson is a trademark of Thomas Nelson, Inc.

Devotions are adapted from *Women of Faith Devotional Bible* © 2010 by Thomas Nelson Publishers, Inc.

Thomas Nelson, Inc., titles may be purchased in bulk for educational, business, fund-raising, or sales promotional use. For information, please e-mail SpecialMarkets@ThomasNelson.com.

ISBN-13: 978-1-4003-1968-8
ISBN-13: 978-1-4003-1967-1 (with display)

Printed in Mexico

12 13 14 15 16 QUAD 5 4 3 2

www.thomasnelson.com

CONTENTS

God has designed a mother's life to be filled with the joy of His presence. When God looks at you, He sees only beauty. He has blessed you with the precious gift of a child. The devotions within this book include Scripture and the writings of twenty-six women who have devoted themselves to living and writing for the glory of God. This book addresses twelve gifts God showers on every mother such as His love, peace, grace, forgiveness, and truth that are essential to your daily walk with Him.

Our hope is that your heart will be touched and your eyes opened by the Savior who loves you with an everlasting love. Allow God to use His words to change your life and inspire your soul.

Charm is deceitful and beauty is passing,
but a woman who fears the LORD,
she shall be praised.
PROVERBS 31:30

❧ Protecting Grace ❧

READ 2 CHRONICLES 16:7–10.

The eyes of the LORD run to and fro through-
out the whole earth, to show Himself strong on
behalf of those whose heart is loyal to Him.
2 CHRONICLES 16:9

*O*ne of the most common responses
my freshmen college students experienced each fall was eagerness to escape
the watchful eyes of their parents. To these
students, leaving home and moving into a
dormitory with other young freedom seek-
ers was a dream come true. In contrast was
the little boy who, after wandering from his
mother's side, soon found himself in the
toy department. His mother rushed over
to him. "Bryan, I've been frantic. I had no
idea where you were!"

Unperturbed, he looked up and said
sweetly, "But, Mama, you always know
where I am. See, you're right here beside me."

For those of us who wander into the toy
department and hope not to be discovered,
remember that God views us through the
lens of grace. That grace seeks to protect us
as well as love us.

Marilyn Meberg

❧ Called to Liberty ❧

READ GALATIANS 5:1–15.

For you, brethren, have been called to liberty;
only do not use liberty as an opportunity for
the flesh, but through love serve one another.
GALATIANS 5:13

Many years ago I learned what it means to be free. Until I went to college, my family had attended a denominational, legalistic church that preached performance. Everything about it encouraged conformity, compliance, and criticism toward those who did not "follow the rules."

While I was away at college, Mother and Daddy changed churches, and upon my first visit, I began to learn the meaning of big biblical words like *predestination*, *justification,* and *sanctification* and how the truth of those meanings work in little words like *peace*, *grace*, and *freedom*.

This free life in Christ permits us to accept and love others just as they are. Not only that, but it encourages us to serve people we don't even know. It can take us to a mission field on the other side of the world or down a dormitory hallway to help someone in need.

Luci Swindoll

✤ Confident Hope ✤

READ 1 PETER 3:15.

> *Sanctify the Lord God in your hearts,*
> *and always be ready to give a defense*
> *to everyone who asks you a reason*
> *for the hope that is in you.*
> 1 PETER 3:15

I'll never forget the time I prayed about whether or not we could adopt a child. In His unmistakable voice, the Lord gave me Proverbs 13:12 as a promise: "When the desire comes, it is a tree of life." Not if, but when! I rested in the hope that God would send us the right child at the right time.

A friend later asked me how I could have such confident hope. "I don't know if my faith is that big," she said.

"The size of my faith doesn't matter," I answered. "I'm confident in the size of my God."

Angela Elwell Hunt

❧ The Joy of My Heart ❧

READ JEREMIAH 15:15–18.

Your words were found, and I ate them, and Your word was to me the joy and rejoicing of my heart; for I am called by Your name, O LORD God of hosts.
JEREMIAH 15:16

When my children were young, they would head straight for the kitchen after walking in the door from school. The work and stress of the day seemed to melt away with one glance at a plate of cookies waiting on the counter.

Jeremiah wrote about similar appetites. He also headed to the "kitchen" to eat—to consume or devour—God's Word. We, too, will know we are walking closely with Him when we find childlike joy in feasting daily, not only on Scripture but also on the knowledge that Someone knows and loves us so much that He leaves us plates of goodies.

Lynda Hunter Bjorklund

❖ Pure Faith ❖

READ 1 PETER 1:6–9.

In this you greatly rejoice . . . that the genuineness of your faith, being much more precious than gold that perishes, though it is tested by fire, may be found to praise, honor, and glory at the revelation of Jesus Christ.
1 PETER 1:6–7

When gold is refined, it is a fiery process that separates what is true from the flaws and impurities that have become one with it. The process is faithful, but it is temporary. We are called to more. We are impressed with gold and fine jewels, but God is blessed by faith that has come through fire hot enough to burn away what cannot last in His kingdom. At times we are so blistered by the blaze that it seems no good can come out of this fire. In those moments, we must hold on by faith to what we know is true. When we cling to Jesus at the height of the inferno, we will see when the furnace has cooled that what is left is faith—pure, genuine, and honoring to Christ.

Sheila Walsh

❧ What Does God See? ❧

READ DEUTERONOMY 10:12–15.

*What does the LORD your God require
of you, but to fear the LORD your God,
to walk in all His ways and to love Him,
to serve the LORD your God with all
your heart and with all your soul?*
DEUTERONOMY 10:12

When I met my husband, Dave, I liked him. As I spent time with him, I got to know him more and more. We talked, laughed, and even cried together, and I realized my "like" had turned into love, and I couldn't get enough of him.

When God surveys our love for Him, I wonder what He sees. Does He find us being in "like" with Him only? Is He sorrowful for what He knows our relationship could be but isn't because of the absence of time together? Is He sad when we talk and laugh and cry only with others? Does He weep when we let the fire of our love grow cold?

Falling in love with God happens through time spent. The more time we spend with Him, the more we fall in love. It's that simple. It's that joyous. It's that wonderful.

Lynda Hunter Bjorklund

✤ The Garden of God ✤

READ EPHESIANS 4:30–32.

Be kind to one another, tenderhearted, forgiving one another, even as God in Christ forgave you.
EPHESIANS 4:32

*H*ere's an exercise: each morning when you wake up, check the fertile soil of your heart to see if any bitter seed has taken root. That friend who betrayed you, the boss who berated you, the husband who barely understands you— bitter seeds will try to take root in every garden. Weeds are like that.

Next do this: for every bitter root that's come up, apply the greatest weed killer of all—forgiveness. To forgive is to cultivate a garden God will delight in, one filled with the flowers of kindness and tenderness.

Karen Kingsbury

❧ The Model of Truth ❧

*I rejoiced greatly when brethren came and
testified of the truth that is in you, just as you
walk in the truth. I have no greater joy than to
hear that my children walk in truth.*
3 JOHN vv. 3–4

When my four-year-old niece, Abbey,
comes to spend the night with me,
we always have so much fun together. We
get excited and say, "We'll have more fun
than a barrel of monkeys!"

We also have our serious moments, often when we read stories or just talk and
pray together. One of the things we talk
and pray about is truth.

I remember the night Abbey said to me,
"I didn't get spanked today."

"Do you usually get spanked?" I asked.

"Only when I sin," she answered. "Like
when I push my brother down or take his
toys." Then she looked me in the eye and
said, "You sin too, Sa-sa, but your sins are
different."

Now that's the truth! And we all need to
take ownership of those sins by admitting,
or confessing, them to God—and sometimes to one another (see James 5:16).

Sara Trollinger

❧ Gifts of the Spirit ❧

READ 1 CORINTHIANS 12:4–11.

There are diversities of gifts, but the same Spirit.
There are differences of ministries, but the same
Lord. And there are diversities of activities, but
it is the same God who works all in all.
1 CORINTHIANS 12:4–6

Spiritual gifts are given to each individual Christian for the common
good. Gifts—as Paul explains in another
part of this letter—are not toys, but rather
tools. The Corinthians, like the baby Christians they were, were playing with their
gifts as if they were playthings instead of
using them to serve others in the church.

Every Christian is gifted. The Spirit will
indicate what our gift is if we ask Him. One
way to really find out is to start serving others, and our spiritual abilities will evidence
themselves!

Jill P. Briscoe

❧ Be a Peacemaker ❧

READ JAMES 3:13–18.

Wisdom that is from above is first pure, then peaceable, gentle, willing to yield, full of mercy and good fruits, without partiality and without hypocrisy. Now the fruit of righteousness is sown in peace by those who make peace.

JAMES 3:17–18

"Hi, Mom." My eight-year-old son skipped across the room and gave me a hug. "Guess what? I was a peacemaker today."

"You were?" My eyebrows raised a notch. "How did that happen?"

Joshua went on to explain that in a lunchtime game of soccer he had scored a goal against the other team. "But the goalie was mad at me, so he pushed me down, but I walked away, and the yard monitor told me I was a peacemaker."

"Josh, honey, how come you walked away? How come you didn't fight back?"

"Because, Mom, I know that boy's dad, and my dad's bigger than his dad." To this day, when I'm troubled by something unfair, I remember that God wants us to be peacemakers and leave the rest to Him. Our Dad's the very biggest Dad of all.

Karen Kingsbury

❖ The One Who Heals ❖

READ ISAIAH 57:15–19.

Thus says the High and Lofty One who inhabits eternity, whose name is Holy: "I dwell in the high and holy place, with him who has a contrite and humble spirit, to revive the spirit of the humble, and to revive the heart of the contrite ones. . . . I have seen his ways, and will heal him; I will also lead him, and restore comforts to him."

ISAIAH 57:15, 18

What a picture of the beauty of God Isaiah offers here! The One who is high and lifted up in glory, whose robe fills the temple (see Isaiah 6:1), is the same God who draws near to the humble and contrite of spirit. Though He is high and holy, He comes alongside broken people who turn to Him.

When life has rolled over you like a dump truck, how do you see God? Is He far removed, waiting for you to get up and dust yourself off? Isaiah declares that God comes near in the moments we would least expect. He breathes new life into our broken places. He takes us by the hand and comforts us. The One who inhabits eternity restores our souls.

Paula Rinehart

⇝ The Creator of All ⇜

READ REVELATION 4:9–11.

You are worthy, O Lord, to receive glory and honor and power; for You created all things, and by Your will they exist and were created.
REVELATION 4:11

*T*his hymn of praise is sung to the Lamb who was slain (see Revelation 5:6), who alone deserves glory, praise, and honor. One day we will cast our earthly achievements at His feet.

Who ever earned a reward without His giving the power to win it? Who ever earned a degree without the given blessing of intelligence? Who ever did the right thing without the moral knowledge written in our conscience and revealed through His Word?

We owe our next breath to His will, our finest hour to His enabling, our little triumphs to His grace. What have we that we have not received? One day we will cast these earthly crowns at His feet where they belong!

We can start practicing now, while we are going about our daily doings. What can you cast at His feet today?

Jill P. Briscoe

❧ Acceptable in Your Sight ❧

READ PSALM 19:12–14.

Let the words of my mouth and the meditation
of my heart be acceptable in Your sight,
O LORD, my strength and my Redeemer.
PSALM 19:14

I love words! In the night they accumulate inside me, and then at daybreak I split open like an overripe watermelon, spewing words like seeds. It is said that women have more words and a greater need to speak them than men. I collect quiet friends for obvious reasons. I can't risk loquacious gals like me, who might suggest I hush up, but those given to silence allow me to speak for both of us. I like that.

So imagine when I stumbled on Psalm 19:14 and realized the words I speak should be acceptable to the Lord. Acceptable? In Hebrew, *acceptable* means "full of favor, kindness, goodwill, and grace." Hmm ... I'd been given to bouts of nitpicking, sporadic sessions of whining, and spouts of vanity. Conversationally, I was at least three quarts low on grace.

With the Lord's help I have given up my endless verbiage (generally) and weigh my words more carefully (usually).

Patsy Clairmont

❧ Boundaries of Freedom ❧

READ 1 PETER 2:13–17.

This is the will of God, that by doing good you may put to silence the ignorance of foolish men—as free, yet not using liberty as a cloak for vice, but as bondservants of God.
1 PETER 2:15–16

I grew up cautious. I lived in mortal fear of getting in trouble. I only remember being in trouble twice in my entire childhood, but I thought I might get in trouble, so I stayed on the safe side.

Luci Swindoll has been good for me. She enjoys tremendous freedom and drags me in that direction all the time. Yet she knows that liberty has God-given boundaries. She understands that in Christ we are free and our freedom enables us to follow Him joyfully. In fact, living in freedom as His bondservant is the only way to stay out of trouble.

Mary Graham

✦ Our Hope Is Jesus ✦

READ 1 PETER 1:3–5.

Blessed be the God and Father of our Lord Jesus
Christ, who according to His abundant mercy
has begotten us again to a living hope through
the resurrection of Jesus Christ from the dead.
1 PETER 1:3

*J*esus established hope on the cross
and forever wrote it into history. How
do we know hope is alive? Because Christ
is alive.

I have analyzed no other topic more
than the one of hope. Without hope, without dreams, we wither and die. I have come
to believe it is the number one reason so
many walk around as depressed believers.
We have consciously and subconsciously
put our hope in things of this world. All of
those things eventually die—each and every one. When they die, we feel the loss.

Hope in Christ, however, is fully alive. It
will never die. Think about that . . . a hope
that can never be silenced. It's an eternal
flame that will never be extinguished. It's
living now, and the inheritance it estab-
lishes is reserved in the heavenly realms.
Look skyward and hope again. Watch Him
move on your behalf.

Kathy Troccoli

✵ Gladness, Joy, and Honor ✵

READ ESTHER 8:7–17.

*The city of Shushan rejoiced and was glad.
The Jews had light and gladness, joy and honor.
And in every province and city, wherever the
king's command and decree came, the Jews
had joy and gladness, a feast and a holiday.*
ESTHER 8:15–17

Wow! "Light and gladness, joy and honor." What a combination! If you have just *one* of those qualities going for you, it's a pretty good day, but to have "light and gladness, joy and honor" working for you is almost too much to contemplate. The grand question is, "How can you have those four qualities in your life at one time?" Those four words seem so splendid when life can be so daily. I believe the order of these words is no mistake because the process has to begin somewhere, so light is the starting point. If you want your life to be marked with gladness, joy, and honor, you have to have light. Jesus said, "I am the light of the world" (John 8:12). So when Jesus is in your life, you see things differently because you have light. The dark places that trouble you are illumined, and you look at them differently. You see that you are never alone.

Jan Silvious

Lovingkindness
❧ in the Morning ❧

READ PSALM 143:5–8.

*Cause me to hear Your lovingkindness
in the morning, for in You do I trust;
cause me to know the way in which I
should walk, for I lift up my soul to You.*
PSALM 143:8

*E*ach morning we get to choose what
will be the first thing we take into our
hearts. We can switch on the television and
hear of wars and rumors of wars, of human
suffering and moral decay, or we can bathe
ourselves—heart and soul—in the Word of
God. We can't isolate ourselves from what
is going on around us every day, but we can
decide who has the first word.

We can look at our relationship with
God through the lens of our culture, or we
can look at our culture through the lens of
God's Word. The first would seek to erode
faith in a God we cannot see. But the latter
builds on a firm foundation of what is eternally true and points us to our God, who
remains faithful and will continue to be so
all the days of our lives.

Sheila Walsh

❧ A Garment of Love ❧

READ PROVERBS 10:12.

Hatred stirs up strife, but love covers all sins.
PROVERBS 10:12

*I*t is easy to love the friend who is our encourager, standing on the sideline of life, cheering us on. We elevate people's value to us based upon how they make us feel about ourselves. To the booing section, those criticizing types who seem to delight in our mistakes, we withdraw our fondness. When we practice the act of love, covering up the ugly things said against us as though the offending tongue had simply made an innocent slip, we find the gentle garment of love draped over our own mistakes. Christ does this for us continually, covering us with the beauty of His own righteousness. Love is the act of sharing our undeserved covering, even with those who are not so lovable. Not only is unrequited love our responsibility; it is also our privilege as children of the King.

Patricia Hickman

⁎ The Treasure of Forgiveness ⁎

READ MARK 11:25–26.

"And whenever you stand praying,
if you have anything against anyone,
forgive him, that your Father in heaven
may also forgive you your trespasses."
MARK 11:25

*T*hrough my children, I have learned that forgiveness is not free—it costs the one who forgives. When my children were young, the cost of forgiving their mishaps was small—the disappointment of a shattered vase, the effort of scrubbing a crayon-scribbled wall, the embarrassment of correcting a childish lie. As my children grew older, however, I paid for their mishaps with the agony of an aching heart.

And then I realized how much my own failings cost my heavenly Father. I am older now—and supposedly wiser—so when I fail, my loving Father's heart aches on my account. How can I not extend the treasure of forgiveness to others when God so richly extends it to me?

Angela Elwell Hunt

❖ Robe of Righteousness ❖

READ JOSHUA 24:14–15.

*Fear the LORD, serve Him in sincerity
and in truth, and put away the gods which
your fathers served on the other side of the
River and in Egypt. Serve the LORD!*
JOSHUA 24:14

*M*y three-year-old is at the stage
where he likes to dress himself.
Every morning he'll choose a mismatched
ensemble from his drawers and pull it on
right over his footed pajamas. He'll arrive
at breakfast in bulky layers, only to be sent
back upstairs to set things right.

Sometimes we do the same thing. We
try to hang on to our favorite PJs when
the Lord is asking us to trade them in for
a robe of righteousness. Joshua needed to
urge the children of Israel to put away their
false gods. If you were truthful with yourself—and with God—would you need to
put away something as well?

Christa Kinde

❧ Let Your Light Shine ❧

READ MATTHEW 5:13–16.

> *"Let your light so shine before men, that*
> *they may see your good works and*
> *glorify your Father in heaven."*
> MATTHEW 5:16

The basic purpose for living is to glorify our Father in heaven. We who believe in Him are lights on a hillside, seen from a distance. We are to cast vision, give warmth, and show a better way to those living in darkness. In short, God instructs us to shine. How do we do that?

Encourage instead of criticize. Love instead of hate. Hope instead of doubt. Give instead of take. Trust instead of worry.

We open our hearts to others so they will be prompted to open their hearts to God. Encouragement, love, hope, generosity, and trust are all gifts of God by the work of His Spirit. They don't spring from our humanity; they spring from His grace. God gives the light. He uses us to show the way. And He is glorified. What a high calling and wonderful purpose to be on this earth!

Luci Swindoll

❧ Deep Roots ❧

READ PSALM 4:6–8.

I will both lie down in peace, and sleep; for You alone, O LORD, make me dwell in safety.
PSALM 4:8

*I*n north Georgia where my family and I live, the landscape displays tall Georgia pine trees. While the stately tree is beautiful, during even the mildest storm our yards and streets are littered with tree limbs.

The landscape in south Georgia is different though. Along the balmy coast stands the stately palm tree. This tree is not the least bit moved by the threat of strong winds. You see, the palm tree's trunk and deep root system allow it to bend but not break. It possesses great resistance and resilience, even in the fiercest storm.

When the Word of God is in you, you don't have to worry about life's storms. You can even lie down at night and rest peacefully, knowing that God is in control. Your heavenly Father will be up all night, so you, my friend, might as well get some sleep.

Babbie Mason

❖ God's Way ❖

READ PSALM 147:2–6.

The LORD . . . heals the brokenhearted
and binds up their wounds.
PSALM 147:2–3

What is healing really? Our society tells us healing exists mostly in the physical realm. The Bible tells us it exists first in the heart. A friend of mine recently succumbed to cancer after a ten-year battle. Throughout the final months of her life, she continued to maintain that God had indeed healed her. Her understanding of eternity and her place in God's design was deeper than ever before in her life. The physical aspects of the disease were secondary to that. Her humility and wisdom taught me much about God's healing and His character. God will heal you.

Kathy Troccoli

❧ A High Position ❧

READ REVELATION 1:4–8.

To Him who loved us and washed us from our
sins in His own blood, and has made us kings
and priests to His God and Father, to Him
be glory and dominion forever and ever.
REVELATION 1:5–6

*A*s I meditate on this powerful greeting John gives to the seven churches, I find that I must fall on my knees in praise and adoration of our Lord. Christ's love cannot be doubted. He sacrificed His sinless life in order to cleanse us from our sinfulness. He who is the King of kings and our great High Priest graces us with dignity by exalting us to the position of kings and priests.

And what should be our response to such love? A life lived in holiness, in kingly victory over the world, and in consecrated service to the One whose love is without end. To Him be the glory!

Cynthia Heald

❧ A Sun and a Shield ❧

READ PSALM 84:10–11.

*The LORD God is a sun and shield; the LORD
will give grace and glory; no good thing will
He withhold from those who walk uprightly.*
PSALM 84:11

I'm embarrassed at how often I've
heard myself say, "Oh, God, *please*."
I learned to beg with my mother, so I em-
ploy those same techniques with God. To
my relief, it never works. You see, God's
Word says He is a sun and a shield. A sun
provides light so we can see. And a shield
protects us from what we can't see. He has
the grace to give us both.

I've learned God is *full* of grace. He with-
holds nothing that is good for me. I walk
with Him; He shows me the way. I have
a need; He provides it. When it isn't the
fulfillment of my own imaginings, I trust
Him. He sees the end from the beginning.
He has the grace to give me what I need—
and the grace to not. He's *full* of grace.

Mary Graham

⊹ Redeem It ⊹

READ RUTH 4:1–10.

If you will redeem it, redeem it;
but if you will not redeem it, then tell me,
that I may know; for there is no one but you
to redeem it, and I am next after you.
RUTH 4:4

*B*oaz, a good man, loved Ruth and longed to marry her. The problem was, according to the law, someone else was first in line. Widows were destitute in those days, but a near relative could purchase the land she had lost when her husband died, marry her, and provide for her. Boaz was a relative, but the other guy was a nearer relative, and he was a cad! He wanted the land but cared nothing for Ruth. If Ruth had hurried into this marriage, she might have ended up with the cad, but she listened to Naomi, who advised, "Sit still, my daughter, until you know how the matter will turn out" (Ruth 3:18).

How many young women have failed to listen to their parents or godly older mentors and then had great regrets? If God is in it, He will keep it together. Trust God enough to give it time.

Dee Brestin

❖ Christ Our Hope ❖

READ HEBREWS 10:19–25.

Let us hold fast the confession
of our hope without wavering,
for He who promised is faithful.
HEBREWS 10:23

*A*uthentic hope is not dependent on what we hope for but on the One we hope in. Circumstances always change, but Christ alone is unchanging. When He is the object of our hope, we will not be shaken; but when we rely on people or events to secure our hope, we will continually find ourselves walking on shifting, sinking sand. The Scripture says that hope does not disappoint; therefore, we can confidently trust Christ, our hope and the anchor for our souls—sure and steadfast.

Heather Mercer

❧ The Joyful Sound ❧

READ PSALM 89:15–18.

Blessed are the people who know the
joyful sound! They walk, O LORD, in
the light of Your countenance.
In Your name they rejoice all day long.
PSALM 89:15–16

*E*very now and then, when things aren't going right, I check out what I'm listening to. What does the background of my life sound like? Television sitcoms? News reports? Gossip? Grumbling? If I can answer yes to any of those, then usually I presume a correlation, and I do my best to change the station to one that shouts out joy.

We tend to think our day is shaped by what we think, see, and do. But the sound of our lives is equally important. On those days when the background noise of my life isn't what it should be, I slip in a worship CD, listen for the giggle of my young son, or concentrate on the still small voice of God encouraging me, leading me on. All of these are joyful sounds, and with them I'll walk in the light of God's countenance.

Karen Kingsbury

✶ A Changed Life ✶

READ LUKE 18:1–8.

Then the Lord said, "Hear what the unjust judge said. And shall God not avenge His own elect who cry out day and night to Him, though He bears long with them? I tell you that He will avenge them speedily. Nevertheless, when the Son of Man comes, will He really find faith on the earth?"
LUKE 18:6–8

Faith is the persuasion that something is true, and that persuasion is so strong that it results in a changed life. So when you are a woman of faith, you are totally convinced that what God says is true, and that governs how you live! That means not only that you believe but also that your belief changes your life.

It wasn't until I truly came to faith through a relationship with Jesus Christ that my life changed. Faith gave me an understanding of God that altered how I behaved. As a result, faith changed my lifestyle. It began to govern how I lived. Now I have a faith I know is real because it has been tried and has stood the test. How's your faith today? Will it stand? God longs for you to trust Him.

Jan Silvious

❧ With All Your Strength ❧

READ MARK 12:28–34.

"'You shall love the LORD your God with all your heart, with all your soul, with all your mind, and with all your strength.' This is the first commandment. And the second, like it, is this: 'You shall love your neighbor as yourself.'"

MARK 12:30–31

*T*he first *commandment* came after the first *commitment*. In the beginning God loved us first. When we understand His love for us, we don't have to be commanded to love Him; we simply respond to what He has already given. Second, we give away what we have been given. Everything flows from God's loving the world first. We love Him in return and love others with the overflow of His love. Without God loving us first, there would be nothing to respond to, and there would be no overflow. He started it flowing down; we stand under the waterfall to receive and then share.

Nicole Johnson

✦ Confess with Your Mouth ✦

READ ROMANS 10:9–10.

*If you confess with your mouth the Lord Jesus and
believe in your heart that God has raised Him
from the dead, you will be saved. For with the heart
one believes unto righteousness, and with
the mouth confession is made unto salvation.*
ROMANS 10:9–10

This passage directs our actions toward two significant verbs: *confess* and *believe*. Confession can be to acknowledge. In Mark 1:5 the people were "confessing their sins," acknowledging they were sinners.

Confession can also be an admission of truth. "Through the proof of this ministry, they glorify God for the obedience of your confession to the gospel of Christ" (2 Corinthians 9:13). So when we confess, we admit the fact of our sin's presence and the forgiveness of it through Jesus.

To believe is to consider something to be true or honest. When you believe that Jesus is truly God's Son, risen to life after death on the cross for sin, and then acknowledge and confess sin as well as your need for Him, the good news is that "you will be saved." How are you saved? Through confession and belief.

Marilyn Meberg

☙ Declaring Righteousness ☙

READ PROVERBS 12:17–22.

*He who speaks truth declares righteousness, but
a false witness, deceit. . . . The tongue
of the wise promotes health. The truthful
lip shall be established forever, but
a lying tongue is but for a moment.*
PROVERBS 12:17–19

*H*ave you ever known a smorgasbord
Christian? Along their journey they
say, "I'll take a little of that and a small
helping of this. I'd like a big portion of this,
but you can keep that."

When it comes to walking with God,
there are no options. You give Him your all,
or you give Him nothing at all. You either
embrace the truth, or you live a lie. The
truth does not conform to situational eth-
ics or political correctness. We conform to
truth. The Lord delights in those who love
truth, speak truth, and live truth.

Babbie Mason

✦ Live for the Lord ✦

READ MARK 8:34–38.

*"What will it profit a man if he gains
the whole world, and loses his own soul?"*
MARK 8:36

In 2002, Heather Mercer and Dayna Curry, two young American women who had been imprisoned in Afghanistan by the Taliban forces, joined Women of Faith for several weekends. Heather described her fear as she sat on the floor of their prison cell listening to bombs drop, coming closer and closer each time. She was afraid. She didn't want to die on the other side of the world so far away from home.

As bombs dropped and machine-gun fire was heard in the streets of Kabul, there was an internal war that was just as real, just as deadly. Finally, this text burst the dam of fear and uncertainty: "What will it profit a man if he gains the whole world, and loses his own soul? Or what will a man give in exchange for his soul?" (Mark 8:36–37).

Heather wrote in her journal that if she lived she would live for the Lord, and if she died she would die for the Lord. With that declaration firmly established, she experienced a deep peace and rest.

Sheila Walsh

✦ Keeping Watch ✦

READ PROVERBS 16:7.

*When a man's ways please the LORD, He makes
even his enemies to be at peace with him.*
PROVERBS 16:7

Women thrive on relationships. Even as little girls, we grow up wanting people to like us. Do you remember the uncomfortable feeling back in elementary school when someone just looked at you wrong? As adults we're still uneasy when we feel that others have something against us—whether it is the client, the boss, the co-worker, or the neighbor.

Whatever the reason—jealousy, greed, prejudice—enemies surface from cradle to grave. But the good news is they don't have to destroy us. They don't even have to make us uneasy. God says, "Please Me, and I'll keep watch over your shoulder"—a very good feeling in today's world.

Dianna Booher

❧ Health to Your Flesh ❧

READ PROVERBS 3:7–8.

*Do not be wise in your own eyes; fear the
LORD and depart from evil. It will be health
to your flesh, and strength to your bones.*
PROVERBS 3:7–8

"Most people suffer poor health," the old
saying goes, "not because of what
they eat but because of what is eating them!"

Years before science linked healthy bodies and healthy minds, Solomon wrote that
humility, reverence, and righteous living
would result in physical health. Grocery
store newsstands abound with magazines
to promote a healthy lifestyle, but how
many of those consider a person's spiritual
well-being?

• *Feeling stressed?* Cast your cares upon
the One who cares for you (1 Peter 5:7).

• *Exhausted?* Run to the One whose yoke
is easy and burden is light (Matthew 11:30).

• *Worried?* Place your concerns in Jesus'
hands, and trust Him to meet your needs
(Matthew 6:25–26).

Center your life on the will of God, and
you'll soon realize that the trouble with
most people is not that they are all rundown but that they are all wound up!

Angela Elwell Hunt

❧ A Living Sacrifice ❧

READ ROMANS 12:1–2.

I beseech you therefore, brethren, by the mercies of God, that you present your bodies a living sacrifice, holy, acceptable to God, which is your reasonable service. And do not be conformed to this world, but be transformed by the renewing of your mind, that you may prove what is that good and acceptable and perfect will of God.
ROMANS 12:1–2

Before getting out of bed I often pray, "Lord, I present my body as a living and holy sacrifice to You. Help me to do Your will today." It is important for me, early in the day, to set my mind on the eternal and to surrender my body in order to walk in a way that would please God.

As I become a living sacrifice committed to holiness and spiritual transformation, I cannot help but *prove*—demonstrate, manifest—the will of God, which He intends for my good, and when I am consecrated is acceptable and perfect.

Cynthia Heald

❧ You Have the Light ❧

READ JOHN 12:27–36.

*Jesus said to them, "A little while longer
the light is with you. Walk while you have
the light, lest darkness overtake you; he who
walks in darkness does not know where he is
going. While you have the light, believe in the
light, that you may become sons of light."*
JOHN 12:35–36

With the Spirit of God in our hearts,
we have the ability to reflect light—
the light of Jesus Christ.

When you were a child holding a mirror in your hand, if you caught the glint of the sun, that mirror reflected a beam that could actually illumine a dark place. It was better than holding a flashlight because the reflection source was from above you, not from batteries in your hand.

By the same token, we carry this kind of ability inside us when we walk in Jesus' light. This light shows up in different forms—humor, kindness, peace, hope, grace—characteristics that can come out of us when the light Source shines through us.

Darkness is scary, yet millions of people have no one to help them see the way out. Jesus instructs us to become "sons of light."

Luci Swindoll

❖ Run with Endurance ❖

READ HEBREWS 12:1–2.

*Since we are surrounded by so great a cloud
of witnesses, let us lay aside every weight,
and the sin which so easily ensnares us,
and let us run with endurance the race
that is set before us, looking unto Jesus,
the author and finisher of our faith.*
HEBREWS 12:1–2

During my four years of high school, I ran track and cross-country. I trained three hours per day. I trained to win. When race day came, I was ready. Standing on the starting line, gun ready to fire, adrenaline pumping, I occasionally wondered, *Can I really do this?* Then I would look up and see the crowds and my teammates ready to cheer me on.

In Christ we've been called to run a wonderful race—a race to pursue His presence and His purposes. Sin keeps us from being able to run that race the way God intended. Let us follow Christ's example and turn away from any vice that keeps us from running well. Dear saint, do not give up! Run, run, run! Jesus Himself sits among the great crowd cheering you on!

Heather Mercer

❧ The Way up Is Down ❧

READ 1 PETER 5:5–7.

Humble yourselves under the mighty hand of
God, that He may exalt you in due time, casting
all your care upon Him, for He cares for you.
1 PETER 5:6–7

*H*ave you discovered that God's way
up is down? Peter learned that truth
the hard way—and he wanted to make sure
we understand as well! To humble yourself
is to surrender to the authority of God in
your life. "Okay, Lord, I give in. You know
what is best for me." There is something
enormously freeing about a humility that
recognizes and surrenders to God—as God.

I think of God's authority in my life as
if I'm standing directly under the shower
of His blessing. I want to be there with
my face turned upward, soaking in all He
pours out, letting my cares fall away. Peter
seemed to say that hope is birthed in this
very place. As I rest under the mighty hand
of God, I let Him carry the weight of my
life. My hope is planted in the reality that
He cares for me—pure and simple.

Paula Rinehart

✤ He Will Save Us ✤

READ ISAIAH 25:6–9.

> *"Behold, this is our God; we have waited*
> *for Him, and He will save us. . . . We will*
> *be glad and rejoice in His salvation."*
> ISAIAH 25:9

Social activities were sparse in the small town where I grew up. Our only entertainment outside the home was at school or church. In fact, I thought both were primarily places for social gatherings.

In college I felt alone. Away from home, without my family or friends, I struggled until I met students whose hearts were aflame with the joy of the Lord. They had personal, meaningful relationships with God.

I was amazed! Ultimately, I came to Christ and experienced that same joy. I have been rejoicing ever since. I didn't know what I longed for, but it was Him and His joy.

Mary Graham

⟡ Never-Ending Faith ⟡

READ HEBREWS 11:1–3.

Now faith is the substance of things hoped for,
the evidence of things not seen.
HEBREWS 11:1

*T*he writer to the Hebrews gifted us with an eloquent discourse on faith—what faith looks like and how faith acts.

In Hebrews 11, we are told that faith in God is being sure of what we hope for. That is the reality of the Christian life. We know whom we have believed in, even though we have never seen Him. Our hope is in Christ, and because of that it is a sure thing. Hope on its own has no power. I can hope to wake up one morning and be three inches taller than the night before, but that hope would not serve me well. Hope depends on what it is linked to.

Our hope in Christ is surer than anything we can see and experience on this earth, and we arrive at that place through faith. Faith is a living thing. It is our lifestyle. It is a commitment to walk in the footsteps of Christ, not knowing what lies ahead but knowing that He is with us. Therefore we can take the next step.

Sheila Walsh

⟿ Unconditional Love ⟿

READ 1 CORINTHIANS 16:13–14.

Watch, stand fast in the faith, be brave, be strong. Let all that you do be done with love.
1 CORINTHIANS 16:13–14

*M*y dad is one of my heroes. Last year, during one of my greatest personal trials, my dad displayed a measure of love that reminds me of Christ Himself. During my 105 days of incarceration in a Taliban prison, my father worked tirelessly to secure my release. Every day he talked with government officials, was interviewed by countless reporters, and negotiated with members of the Taliban. As the situation in Afghanistan escalated, no one knew what our fate was to be.

Amid the chaos, my father announced his desire to take my place in prison and pay the penalty for the crime for which my friends and I were being accused. Knowing the potential severity of my sentence, my father loved me enough to give his life in exchange for mine. I did not deserve the gift he was willing to give or the sacrifice he was willing to make, but love compelled him to do whatever it took to set me free. So it is with the love of Christ.

Heather Mercer

❖ All Want Forgiveness ❖

READ PSALM 103:1–5.

Bless the LORD, O my soul, and forget not all His benefits: who forgives all your iniquities, who heals all your diseases, who redeems your life from destruction, who crowns you with lovingkindness and tender mercies.
PSALM 103:2–4

*O*ne of my favorite definitions of *forgiveness* is "giving up your right to punish." That always seemed to make good sense to me because my natural bent when hurt is to punish the one who has done the hurting—until I'm the one in need of forgiveness. Then I really don't want to be reminded of what I've done, and I really don't want to be punished. I want the one who has anything against me to send it away from me and give up her right to punish me.

We all want forgiveness. It is a blessed state. That is why it is so gratifying to know that God has forgiven us. He has sent our offenses far away from us by putting them on His Son, Jesus Christ. He also has given up His right to punish us. We are forgiven. That is what makes us members of His kingdom.

Jan Silvious

⟶ Truth to Overcome ⟵

READ PSALM 51:5–6.

> *You desire truth in the inward parts,*
> *and in the hidden part*
> *You will make me to know wisdom.*
> PSALM 51:6

God desires that we know and practice truth in every area of our lives. If we feel defeated or hopeless because of an addiction, bondage, or sin, we probably don't know the truth of God's Word concerning our problem.

I've learned that if I apply God's truth when I'm struggling, He gives me wisdom to overcome. God's Word promises that when we walk in truth, we will be overcomers. Jesus said the truth will set us free.

God doesn't want us to have intellectual knowledge of truth. He wants us to experience its power operating in our hearts.

Sara Trollinger

❖ God's Purpose for Me ❖

READ VERSES 24–25 OF JUDE.

*Now to Him who is able to keep you from
stumbling, and to present you faultless before
the presence of His glory with exceeding joy,
to God our Savior, who alone is wise,
be glory and majesty, dominion and power,
both now and forever. Amen.*
JUDE vv. 24–25

I have memorized this glorious, comforting benediction. These verses give great security and hope, as I am reminded of God's purpose to protect and to keep His children blameless in this world full of deceivers and mockers.

I am encouraged to know of God's present concern for us, but I am deeply humbled and overwhelmed by His future desire to bring us great joy as we are presented faultless before His glorious presence.

It is no surprise that Jude ends his letter in splendid adoration and worship of our majestic, powerful, and all-wise God. And it is no surprise that having these words in my heart encourages praise to God our Savior.

Cynthia Heald

✤ Peace Is Contagious ✤

READ 1 TIMOTHY 2:1–2.

I exhort first of all that supplications, prayers, intercessions, and giving of thanks be made for all men, for kings and all who are in authority, that we may lead a quiet and peaceable life in all godliness and reverence.
1 TIMOTHY 2:1–2

*E*verybody wants peace, but there seems to be less peace in our world today than ever before. Peace is contagious. You possess it, and others are overwhelmed by it. As the peace of Christ consumes your life, it will influence your home. Your home will impact the street where you live. Your neighborhood will gain a reputation for being a great place to raise a family, impacting the entire community. All over the city, your community will be known as a peaceful place to live. Crime will decrease, and people will be able to walk the streets without fear. Your city will be such a peaceful place to live that people all over the state and the nation will be amazed.

Sound a bit idealistic? Why not give it a try and see what happens? Let the peace of Christ begin with you and start to consume the world in which you live.

Babbie Mason

✦ God Is Gracious ✦

READ JOEL 2:12–27.

*Return to the LORD your God, for He is gracious
and merciful, slow to anger, and of great
kindness; and He relents from doing harm.*
JOEL 2:13

I was born with a pulmonary defect that weakened the muscles around my heart. As my condition worsened, my mother was told that I would die before I started school. But one day, as a new Christian reading her Bible, Mom realized this news was contrary to Scripture she'd read. Mom decided to "spend" God's promises, and she went out and bought my school clothes and enrolled me in kindergarten.

Mom's faith was tested often as I continued to miss many days of school. At some point, however, things turned around, and I grew stronger. By the end of first grade, I had won a physical fitness award. In the years to come, free from all heart problems, I became the biggest tomboy in my family.

We have numerous promises to achieve the abundant life Jesus promised. If it's healing you need today, pray for it with childlike faith.

Lynda Hunter Bjorklund

✤ Citizens of Heaven ✤

READ ISAIAH 9:6–7.

> *For unto us a Child is born, unto us a Son is given; and the government will be upon His shoulder. And His name will be called Wonderful, Counselor, Mighty God, Everlasting Father, Prince of Peace.*
> ISAIAH 9:6

As believers in Jesus, we occupy earth, but we are citizens of heaven. We are only passing through. One day our feet will finally touch our homeland. In that city, under the authority of Christ, there will be no more wars, no more fear, and no more death. There will be no depression, no recession, and no budget woes. No more man against man, fathers against sons, or mothers against daughters. The government that will be upon Christ's shoulders will be ruled by peace. And of His peace there will be no end.

Bow now or bow later. Whether you are considered a king or a commoner, at the name of Jesus, every knee will bow and every tongue will confess that He is Lord of all the lords and King of all the kings. Is He Lord and King in your heart?

Babbie Mason

❧ His Grace Is Sufficient ❧

READ HEBREWS 4:14–16.

*Let us therefore come boldly to the
throne of grace, that we may obtain mercy
and find grace to help in time of need.*
HEBREWS 4:16

*E*very day in Afghanistan, dozens of
widows and orphans approached us
boldly on the street, begging for food,
medicine, or money. Desperate and impov-
erished, these widows and orphans came
to us for support. We loved and cared for
them and always did our utmost to help,
but often our resources were limited.

Like those widows and orphans, we are
spiritual ragamuffins desperately in need of
the grace and mercy of God. It is our life-
line, our spiritual food, an IV to our soul.
Thankfully, the One who sits on the throne
of grace possesses limitless resources, and
He gives them freely; we need only come.

Heather Mercer

✣ Come to the Waters ✣

READ ISAIAH 55:1–5.

Everyone who thirsts, come to the waters;
and you who have no money, come, buy
and eat. Yes, come, buy wine and milk
without money and without price.
ISAIAH 55:1

*H*ave you ever offered to give someone something they needed, but instead of graciously receiving your gift, they
insisted on paying you for it? It is hard to
receive without wanting to "make things
even" with the one who is giving.

Perhaps that is why the divine call of
Isaiah 55:1 has been a stumbling block to
so many. "Surely, I must do something to
receive this salvation. It cannot be free."
But free it is! God does not sell His living
water. Because He knows our inclination to
want to pay, He says, "This is the way you
buy—without money and without price."

Everyone is at liberty to respond to this
gracious invitation to eternal refreshment
and joy.

Cynthia Heald

❖ Resting Securely ❖

READ PSALM 146:5–9.

Happy is he who has the God of Jacob for
his help, whose hope is in the LORD his God,
who made heaven and earth, the sea, and
all that is in them; who keeps truth forever.
PSALM 146:5–6

*T*he psalmist wasn't writing about a wishy-washy hope that might or might not come true. His hope was a certainty, for his faith rested securely in the God of Jacob. The God of Abraham, Isaac, and Jacob—who came to earth as Jesus Christ—fed the hungry, opened blinded eyes, and led sinners to the freedom of repentance and forgiveness.

Do you hope to lead your children to the Lord? Do you hope to reach your neighbors with the love of the gospel? Do you hope to make a difference for Christ in your community? In the world?

Aim high in hope, and make big plans. Work as if everything depends upon you; pray as if everything depends upon God. Then you, too, will be able to say, "I will hope continually, and will praise You yet more and more" (Psalm 71:14).

Angela Elwell Hunt

❧ A Cheerful Heart ❧

READ PROVERBS 15:13.

*A merry heart makes a cheerful countenance,
but by sorrow of the heart the spirit is broken.*
PROVERBS 15:13

*J*oy comes in great variety, but whenever it arrives, it lifts the spirit. A cheerful heart sees us through the tough spots and releases tension in pressure situations. It crosses the barrier of language or culture. It erases stress in business meetings and misunderstandings between friends. It relieves boredom. It makes us laugh.

Laughter is a "reflex luxury," totally unrelated to our struggle for survival. But the service it provides helps our sad hearts get through the day. God gave us the gift of laughter. I love that about Him.

Look for ways today to transform self-pity or bitterness into laughter. Attack the thieves that steal your joy. Savor your moments. Live in the present. Pay attention. Take a few risks. Be intentionally involved. Have fun. You'll be glad you did. Your face will show it.

Luci Swindoll

❖ Stand Firm in Your Faith ❖

READ 2 THESSALONIANS 1:3–8.

We are bound to thank God always for you,
brethren, as it is fitting, because your faith
grows exceedingly, and the love of every one
of you all abounds toward each other.
2 THESSALONIANS 1:3

*T*he conduct of Paul's readers "under fire" triggered a response of immense gratitude to the God who had used Paul as an instrument in their lives. Is there any greater thrill than to help someone to know the Jesus we know and to hear that they are standing firm in their faith?

Most of us do not have a situation as these believers did where our lives are in danger because of the gospel, but we can be "under fire" for other reasons—because of a divorce, ill health, or ridicule for our beliefs.

What an encouragement it must have been for the Thessalonians to receive Paul's letter. Never underestimate the power of prayer or a word of simple encouragement.

Spend a moment asking God if there is a Thessalonian in your life who needs you today.

Jill P. Briscoe

❧ At All Times ❧

READ PROVERBS 17:17.

*A friend loves at all times,
and a brother is born for adversity.*
PROVERBS 17:17

A friend once told me that in life, the circle of friends grows smaller as we get older. "But"—her eyes danced—"those friends who stay are gold—pure gold." I've found that to be so true. Friends I thought would stay by me forever found different paths or allowed walls to come between us.

But a very few friends are pure gold. Friends who understand my crazy writing life. Women I can call after months of good intentions and know I am as loved in that moment as I ever was.

No surprise really when we remember the promise from Proverbs 17:17: a true friend loves at all times, not just for a season. If you have a friend like that, give her a call today, and let her know you love her. Gold friends are one of God's greatest gifts.

Karen Kingsbury

❧ Give It Away ❧

READ 2 CORINTHIANS 2:3–11.

*If anyone has caused grief . . . you ought rather
to forgive and comfort him, lest perhaps such a
one be swallowed up with too much sorrow.*
2 CORINTHIANS 2:5, 7

*T*his week I had lunch with someone
I've needed to forgive. Actually, I had
already chosen forgiveness in my heart and
mind, but it had not been tested. I'd neither
seen nor talked with the person who had
been hurtful to me in a while, and quite
frankly, I was dreading the encounter.

During lunch, out of the blue, I was
overwhelmed with how much God has forgiven me. While I've never deserved forgiveness and had no way to earn it, God in
His grace has forgiven me for everything.
And He does it every time it's needed. As I
sat across the table from my friend, I knew
there was forgiveness in my own heart.
God put it there. All I did was give it away.

Mary Graham

❧ Walk in Truth ❧

READ VERSES 1–6 OF 2 JOHN.

I rejoiced greatly that I have found some of your children walking in truth, as we received commandment from the Father.
2 JOHN vv. 4

"If she tells you something, you can take it to the bank" is a common saying meant to convey that a person's word counts. They don't brag; they don't lie; they don't hedge. It's the truth and nothing but the truth.

Can you imagine having that standard applied to everything in your life—your words, actions, motives, and thoughts? "Walking in truth" encompasses living every standard God has set before us: loving as He loved, showing compassion as He showed compassion, meeting needs as He did, praying as He prayed.

Walking in truth means getting your head out of the clouds and off the pillow so you can be alert to what God's teaching you in every situation and how He wants to use you each day. It's movement with a passion and a purpose.

Dianna Booher

❧ A Future and a Hope ❧

READ JEREMIAH 29:10–14.

*I know the thoughts that I think toward you,
says the LORD, thoughts of peace and not
of evil, to give you a future and a hope.*
JEREMIAH 29:11

Jeremiah 29:10–14 reveals to us the mind of God as He thinks about His children. Amazingly, those thoughts about us produce peace in Him. He is not wringing His hands and fretting about our mindlessness as we veer repeatedly off the path He has determined for our future.

The reason He does not fret is because He is our Father. The Father knows that He has placed within each of His children His Spirit. God never abandons His own Spirit or those of us in whom the Spirit lives.

Sooner or later, the Father knows His child will act upon the inner nudge to call home. When we find ourselves lost and in despair, the Father promises that when we call, He'll answer. He will also listen.

In the listening, the Father doesn't even ask for an explanation. He asks only that we come home.

Marilyn Meberg

✤ With All People ✤

Pursue peace with all people, and holiness,
without which no one will see the Lord.
HEBREWS 12:14

*T*o have peace with God is an incredible gift. That peace, though, should spill over into our relationships, and peace with people is often something we must intentionally pursue, humans being what we are. "As much as depends on you, live peaceably with all men," Paul said (Romans 12:18). The real evidence of knowing Christ shows up in how tenacious we are to love, forgive, and bear with each other.

Paula Rinehart

❧ Lost Sheep Are Important ❧

READ EZEKIEL 34:11–31.

*Thus says the Lord GOD: "Indeed I Myself will
search for My sheep and seek them out. As a
shepherd seeks out his flock . . . so will I seek out My
sheep and deliver them from all the places where
they were scattered on a cloudy and dark day."*
EZEKIEL 34:11–12

Kristy's mother was the principal of a
Christian school. She was a loving
and devoted mother, but it wasn't enough
to prevent her daughter from taking the
wrong path.

Kristy had run away from home, was
taking drugs, and was living with a man on
the streets. The girl was obviously on the
fast road to destruction.

This heartbroken mother and her support
group prayed for God to rescue her daughter. God heard those prayers. He reached
out to Kristy and delivered her from the
dark places where she was hiding. The dark,
cloudy day of Kristy's rebellion and sin was
turned into a day of healing and blessing.

Today she and her husband are mission-
aries, blessing others as they, too, seek out
the lost and hurting and help to shepherd
them back to God.

Sara Trollinger

❧ We Are God's Pleasure ❧

READ EPHESIANS 1:3–6.

*Blessed be the God and Father of our Lord
Jesus Christ, who has blessed us with every
spiritual blessing in the heavenly places in
Christ, just as He chose us in Him before the
foundation of the world, that we should be
holy and without blame before Him in love.*
EPHESIANS 1:3–4

These are some of the richest words in the Bible for the believer in Jesus Christ. Every phrase is yeasty, making it rise off the page . . . edible in content. It's the universal church in a nutshell, chosen before the world was formed, whose recipients were destined to be children of God. If this isn't sovereignty to the max, I don't know what is.

When we read, "according to the good pleasure of His will" (Ephesians 1:5), that means God had us in mind before time began because He wanted to. It gave Him pleasure to think about us and pour out His grace on us.

We'll never understand this kind of love. It's a wonderful mystery, so I suggest we simply revel in it. We're accepted in God's beloved Son, and there's nothing we can do to change that. God did it. We believe it. It's a done deal. Enjoy it!

Luci Swindoll

❧ Seasoned with Salt ❧

READ COLOSSIANS 4:2–6.

Let your speech always be with grace,
seasoned with salt, that you may know
how you ought to answer each one.
COLOSSIANS 4:6

We understand God's grace for us: undeserved pardon, pure and simple. But guess what? It's the same thing when we interact with others. Instead of jumping into a conversation with a pointed finger and angry eyes, sit back and listen. Give people the benefit of the doubt, and be kind with your words.

Most of our heated conversations would be a whole lot cooler if we got a grip on grace. Go out and make it a point today that whoever you talk to or come across will know the grace of God because they saw a glimpse of it in you.

Karen Kingsbury

❧ Abide in My Word ❧

READ JOHN 8:31–36.

*Jesus said to those Jews who believed Him,
"If you abide in My word, you are My disciples
indeed. And you shall know the truth,
and the truth shall make you free."*
JOHN 8:31–32

Knowing the truth in Christ, who is the truth, is an even greater liberty than we might imagine. We are invited to know Jesus, who is eternally true, but Christ also wants us to face all that is true about ourselves. When by His love we bring who we really are into His light, we are set free from the condemning voices that live in the shadows. Our culture tells us that we are only as sick as our secrets, but where do we take our secrets? We take them to Christ who knows them already and longs to set us free. Do you feel unworthy to come into His presence because of who you are in the quiet recesses of your mind? Christ knows all of that, and still He says, "Come!"

Sheila Walsh

✦ Trees by the Waters ✦

READ JEREMIAH 17:7–8.

Blessed is the man who trusts in the LORD,
and whose hope is the LORD. For he shall be
like a tree planted by the waters . . . and will
not be anxious in the year of drought,
nor will cease from yielding fruit.
JEREMIAH 17:7–8

You and I are like the trees. Without the life-giving power of Jesus Christ, we would dry up.

I went on vacation one year and forgot to leave instructions for a friend to water my favorite tree—a miniature lilac planted on the west side of the house. I told my neighbor, "Be sure to water my tomatoes and flowers," but I forgot to mention the tender tree. When we got back, the little tree sort of resembled the Sahara desert—during a blight.

Jeremiah reminds us that we are blessed (or happy) when we put our hope and trust in the Lord. For then we will be like trees that are planted next to the water—sending our roots deep into the riverbed of God's Word, drawing the thirst-quenching, life-sustaining truth from the flow of His Spirit. Then and only then can we bear fruit so that others will be nourished.

Lori Copeland

❧ Ransomed by Jesus ❧

READ ISAIAH 51:10–11.

*The ransomed of the LORD shall return,
and come to Zion with singing, with everlasting
joy on their heads. They shall obtain joy and
gladness; sorrow and sighing shall flee away.*
ISAIAH 51:11

*C*an you think of someone in your life
who has joy? I met someone recently
whose body radiated joy. If someone had
not told me, I never would have known she
had three terminal diseases. Her life wasn't
pain-free, but she had complete joy. Our
first conversation explained why. She was
in love with Jesus.

My friend had been ransomed! She realized exactly what Jesus had done for her
and knew there would come a time when
sorrow and sighing would flee away. In
Luke 2:10, the angel says, "I bring you good
tidings of great joy." What was this joy? It
was Jesus! You, too, have been ransomed
by Jesus—the only One who could possibly
save you.

Denise Jones

❧ Walk by Faith ☙

READ 2 CORINTHIANS 5:6–8.

We walk by faith, not by sight.
2 CORINTHIANS 5:7

These seven little words describe an entire way of life. To operate in faith instead of based on what we see calls for an inner conviction that God can be trusted to do what He says. When our health is uncertain, He's our Physician. When we're down to our last dime, He's our Provider. When there's no energy, He's our Power. When the Enemy surrounds us, He's our Protector.

If we trust God to do what He says, then we have to trust His timing as well. This is hard for us planners. We prefer circumstances, people, and events to work on our timetable. This way we have the illusion that we're in control!

God has to remind us all the time: If I'm your Physician, Provider, Power, and Protector, don't you think you can trust Me to be your Planner as well?

Luci Swindoll

❧ Abound in Love ❧

READ 1 THESSALONIANS 3:11–13.

May the Lord make you increase and abound
in love to one another and to all.
1 THESSALONIANS 3:12

*I*t was a privilege to grow up surrounded by my mother's friends. Because she had eight children, she didn't go
places to visit. Her friends came to her, and
I listened to their conversations.

Those wonderful women modeled a
caring Christlike community. When anyone was sick or in trouble or when there
was a death in the family, my mother and
her friends rallied to provide whatever was
needed: a meal, a helping hand, a listening
ear. They were a blessing in one another's
lives. They demonstrated love, which
through the years increased. Even today
their influence shapes me.

Mary Graham

❧ How Often, Lord? ❧

READ MATTHEW 18:21–35.

> *Peter came to Him and said, "Lord, how
> often shall my brother sin against me,
> and I forgive him? Up to seven times?" Jesus
> said to him, "I do not say to you, up to seven
> times, but up to seventy times seven."*
> MATTHEW 18:21–22

*H*ow often shall my brother sin against
me? That is the question in our hearts
whenever someone wrongs us. *How long
do I have to let this go on? When is enough
really enough?* We desperately want to show
we have done our part and then draw a line
in the sand. Unfortunately, Jesus won't allow
it. He redefines what our part is. He leads
us gently back to realize how desperately we
need forgiveness. He casts us in the story as
the one who is in great debt, that we might
find new strength to forgive another. How
can we not forgive when we remember all
that He has forgiven us? Whenever we have
trouble extending grace and forgiveness, we
can go back to our fresh need to find grace
and discover there is enough to give away.

Nicole Johnson

✴ Great and Marvelous ✴

READ REVELATION 15:2–4.

Great and marvelous are Your works, Lord God Almighty! Just and true are Your ways, O King of the saints! Who shall not fear You, O Lord, and glorify Your name? For You alone are holy. For all nations shall come and worship before You, for Your judgments have been manifested.
REVELATION 15:3–4

Too many Christians have decided the Bible is true because they believe it. Let other people choose whatever gods they will; we have chosen to believe in Holy Scripture. Unfortunately, we often forget that the Bible is true whether we believe it or not. It is true for the atheist down the street, the orphan wandering a Calcutta alley, and the terrorists who committed suicide on 9/11.

Sincere people can place their faith in falsehood. And sincere people who reject truth do not invalidate it.

Truth—which the Word of God is— stands forever.

One day the people of all nations will bow before Jesus' throne. Truth and falsehood will be revealed. Until then, study and cling to the truth of His Word.

Angela Elwell Hunt

✦ In Every Good Work ✦

READ HEBREWS 13:20–21.

May the God of peace . . . make you complete
in every good work to do His will, working
in you what is well pleasing in His sight.
HEBREWS 13:20–21

*G*od does nothing without purpose. He made each of us with a specific purpose in mind. He also promised to work in us to fulfill that purpose.

It is that promise that keeps me going at House of Hope. Many times I see no possible way to accomplish what God is calling me to do. Those are the times when God draws me into intimacy with Him. He shows me the areas that need perfecting so I can walk in obedience to His purpose for my life. God's purpose for us is that we fulfill His perfect will.

Sara Trollinger

➵ The Author of Peace ➵

READ 1 CORINTHIANS 14:26–35.

*God is not the author of confusion but of peace,
as in all the churches of the saints.*
1 CORINTHIANS 14:33

*P*aul's whole context is orderly conduct in the church and how disorder does not reflect the person and character of God. God is a God of order, and we, His people, should reflect Him.

As people walk through the doors of our churches, are they met with confusion or with harmony and peace? There is enough confusion in the world without having it in the church. We should realize that people are desperately seeking a safe haven for their lives.

Each individual Christian is responsible for peace and harmony in her own heart, which should influence a hectic and confused world.

Jill P. Briscoe

✦ Precious Words of Praise ✦

READ EPHESIANS 4:25–29.

Let no corrupt word proceed out of your mouth,
but what is good for necessary edification,
that it may impart grace to the hearers.
EPHESIANS 4:29

We love to be around those people who have disciplined their mouths to lift us, the hearers, out of our unawareness. They are the lights on a summer night for which we run around with our jars hoping to capture a glimmer of their wisdom. We walk away from them changed, wiser. With a few well-placed words they have shone a light into a place we didn't know was dark. They make us want to be better humans. We covet their radiance and pray it will rise inside of us—and then spread like mad!

Patricia Hickman

❧ Great and Mighty God ❧

READ JEREMIAH 33:1–3.

> "Call to Me, and I will answer you,
> and show you great and mighty things,
> which you do not know."
> JEREMIAH 33:3

There is hardly a truth of Scripture more comforting than the utter, complete, inexhaustible sovereignty of God. Jeremiah often returns to this theme in his book. "Ah, Lord GOD! Behold, You have made the heavens and the earth by Your great power and outstretched arm. There is nothing too hard for You" (32:17).

"Our God Reigns" is a song we often sing—and indeed, He does. His was the first word, and His will be the last. Every big event of history in between, every small detail of our individual lives, takes place under His sovereign care.

Paula Rinehart

✧ Healing of All Kinds ✧

READ MATTHEW 4:23–25.

Jesus went about all Galilee, teaching in their synagogues, preaching the gospel of the kingdom, and healing all kinds of sickness and all kinds of disease among the people.
MATTHEW 4:23

*J*esus healed all kinds of sickness and disease. Many believe that Jesus can heal them but that He may choose not to do so. They believe He may have something for them to learn through their sickness or their sickness is punishment for their sins.

There is some truth in each of these. Jesus still heals, but He may choose not to. Certainly God will use everything for our good and to instruct us—even sickness. And we do reap the consequences of our sin, and sometimes those consequences are sicknesses to which we have exposed ourselves.

Are we any different than those who came to Jesus for healing while He was here on earth? He healed them all. A doctor who helps you get well from skin cancer will tell you to avoid the sun. When Jesus heals you, the Holy Spirit will prompt you to avoid those things that made you sick in the first place. Will you follow His leading?

Vonette Bright

⇝ The Price of Freedom ⇜

READ 2 CORINTHIANS 3:17–18.

> *Now the Lord is the Spirit; and where*
> *the Spirit of the Lord is, there is liberty.*
> 2 CORINTHIANS 3:17

*T*he children of Israel insisted that a veil cover Moses' face to hide the residue of God's glory. They could not get past the rules to take a look at even a speck of God's brilliance. On our behalf, Christ pulled back the veil of legalism that blinded every heart from God's love. Imagine . . . the ancient curtain parts. Behind it awaits our freedom—freedom to approach the Father without a priest, to speak candidly to God in the common language of our hearts. Liberty is our spirits breaking free from man's red tape, skipping happily to the land of grace. There we bask in the sunshine of God's glory. We can see!

Patricia Hickman

✤ Hope of the Glory ✤

READ ROMANS 5:1–5.

Having been justified by faith, we have peace
with God through our Lord Jesus Christ,
through whom also we have access by faith into
this grace in which we stand, and rejoice in hope
of the glory of God. And not only that, but
we also glory in tribulations, knowing that
tribulation produces perseverance; and
perseverance, character; and character, hope.
ROMANS 5:1–4

*E*ugene Peterson says when we live expectantly, "we can't round up enough containers to hold everything God generously pours into our lives" through His Spirit. Hope is our opportunity to look at life with excitement and anticipation. There is something about it that opens the floodgates of heaven. Not only are we the benefactors of His blessing and grace; we're given a chance to grow in the process. Our patience is developed, our character is refined, our minds become more alert, and our eyes stay fixed on the prize. Life is framed through a wide-angle lens. All we have to do is point and shoot in the right direction. Even if we don't get the exact thing we were hoping for, life comes into clearer focus.

Luci Swindoll

❧ Crown of Rejoicing ❦

READ 1 THESSALONIANS 2:17–20.

What is our hope, or joy, or crown of rejoicing?
Is it not even you in the presence of our
Lord Jesus Christ at His coming?
For you are our glory and joy.
1 THESSALONIANS 2:19–20

As a youth pastor's wife, I've wept through more weddings than I can count. Like snapshots, memories of our former students ripple through my mind while I stare at my hands in an effort to avoid outright sobbing.

I don't know how their parents manage to remain calm. I worked with these young people for only a few years, while the parents invested their lives into these children. But they are children no longer. They have embraced a milestone that will alter the course of their futures, and we share in their joy.

One day we, living members of the body of Christ, will greet our heavenly Groom. And I can't help but think that the saints who have gone to heaven before us will be swiping tears of joy from their faces knowing that their work, their prayers, and their teaching have brought us safely to Jesus' side.

Angela Elwell Hunt

✤ Full of Faith and Power ✤

READ ACTS 6:1–8.

> *And they chose Stephen, a man full of*
> *faith and the Holy Spirit. . . . And Stephen,*
> *full of faith and power, did great wonders*
> *and signs among the people.*
> ACTS 6:5, 8

*E*veryone is full of something! Stephen was full of faith and the Holy Spirit's power. Note that he was chosen to serve tables! You need to be full of the Holy Spirit to do that. It takes the fullness of the Spirit to think of others first, to fetch and carry, to humble ourselves to do menial work.

Notice that when people saw the way Stephen served, the word of the Lord spread, and the church grew. Stephen was chosen to serve as surely as Paul was chosen to preach. The result was the same.

Jill P. Briscoe

✦ Walk in Love ✦

READ EPHESIANS 5:1–2.

Walk in love, as Christ also has loved us and given Himself for us, an offering and a sacrifice to God for a sweet-smelling aroma.
EPHESIANS 5:2

*E*very Wednesday afternoon at House of Hope, the teenagers and I have a cozy get-together that we call a fireside chat. The kids love to share from their hearts. Inevitably, in giving their testimonies, they admit they have looked for love in all the wrong places.

Most of these teens don't understand the true meaning of love. They have been brainwashed by TV, movies, magazines, and music that focus on sex. As a result, they end up believing love is supposed to be self-satisfying rather than selfless. They are left empty, hurt, and puzzled after spending money on seductive clothing, sensuous perfumes, feel-good drugs, and perverse one-night stands—all in a futile effort to fill the void inside. Then they learn that their "love tank" becomes full only when they experience the heart change that comes through knowing the love of Jesus Christ, which is free, satisfying, and everlasting.

Sara Trollinger

❖ Blessing of Forgiveness ❖

READ COLOSSIANS 2:11–15.

And you, being dead in your trespasses and the uncircumcision of your flesh, He has made alive together with Him, having forgiven you all trespasses, having wiped out the handwriting of requirements that was against us, which was contrary to us. And He has taken it out of the way, having nailed it to the cross.
COLOSSIANS 2:13–14

Jesus endured the cross so that we could have fellowship with Him and with others through forgiveness—our own as we are forgiven and with others as we forgive. Those we refuse to forgive are seldom more than slightly aware of our unforgiveness, but that unforgiveness destroys our own lives. It robs us of joy, destroys relationships, and makes us physically ill.

When we choose unforgiveness, we put ourselves in bondage to those very people we believe wronged us.

Ask Christ to heal your wounded heart and give you a forgiving heart. Choose Christlikeness—forgiveness. Be in bondage to His peace. Free those you believe have wronged you. Forgive. The feelings and blessings will follow!

Vonette Bright

✻ Knowledge of the Truth ✻

READ 1 TIMOTHY 2:3–7.

*This is good and acceptable in the sight of God
our Savior, who desires all men to be saved
and to come to the knowledge of the truth.*
1 TIMOTHY 2:3–4

When I was younger, before coming to Christ fully, I'd often find myself going head to head with the man I am today married to. Don would present something from the Bible, and I would raise an eyebrow and give a shot at debating what Scripture said.

I laugh today when I think of how I must have sounded. "I know it says that," I'd say, "but I think God wants us to do this," as if my feelings or thoughts could somehow be truth.

God wants us all to be saved, and we cannot do that by creating our own worldview of faith. Salvation is found only by anchoring ourselves to the very Word of God, to His saving truth in Scripture. Today Don and I still study Scripture together, but now there's nothing to debate—God's Word is the truth.

Karen Kingsbury

❧ Wherever You Go ❦

READ JOSHUA 1:7–9.

> *"Be strong and of good courage; do not*
> *be afraid, nor be dismayed, for the LORD*
> *your God is with you wherever you go."*
> JOSHUA 1:9

*M*aybe because I'm the baby of my family, I like being "accompanied." Whether it's a vacation or a trip to the store, you'll hear me say, "Want to come?" I drag people everywhere. It's a great comfort that God is with me wherever I go. His purpose is to stick with me. And mine, to stick with Him. I'm never alone. Sometimes I have to let His Word sink deeply into the recesses of my mind in order to remember. "Lord, thank You that Your Word says You will never leave me or forsake me. Even if I feel forsaken, You are here."

I meditate on verses like that night and day. When I do, I enter into God's perfect plan for my life—His purpose—which is for me to walk with Him, think like He thinks, do what He would do. He accompanies me through life.

Mary Graham

❧ True Peace ❧

READ NUMBERS 6:22–27.

*The LORD bless you and keep you; the LORD
make His face to shine upon you, and be
gracious to you; the LORD lift up His
countenance upon you, and give you peace.*
NUMBERS 6:24–26

*H*umankind defines peace as that moment when all of earth is without strife or war. If that were true, then peace would never find its defining moment here on earth, and the term most certainly would have disappeared from all human language centuries ago, an archaic dream. Peace, then, can only be defined by God, given by Him, and bestowed upon the heart as the crowning prize when every trace of our self has surrendered to the Father's will. When all desire is lost in His, our life becomes a fertile plain—our heart the happy picking ground with peace the bounteous crop. It is upon this single plain of surrender that we can know true peace. It is the royal mark of our adoption, legally sealed by the blood of God's Son, Jesus Christ.

Patricia Hickman

⚜ Covenant of Mercy ⚜

READ DEUTERONOMY 7:12–15.

*The LORD your God will keep with
you the covenant and the mercy which
He swore to your fathers. . . . And the LORD
will take away from you all sickness, and will
afflict you with none of the terrible diseases
of Egypt which you have known.*
DEUTERONOMY 7:12, 15

*I*n ancient Egypt, there were some un-
pleasant diseases: boils, eye afflictions,
and bowel problems. The covenant God had
made with Israel promised them that their
health would be dependent upon their obedience to God. There was God's part, and there
was their part.

This does not mean that our obedience
as people of God earns us divine blessing,
as we live "life after the Fall" with a sinful
nature. Disobedience and sin in the larger
population affect us all as well. We do not
live in a perfect world.

God wants each member of His family to
live within the boundaries He has set for human behavior. He set them in order to bless
us. What family doesn't benefit from patience,
kindness, a readiness to put things right, and
the determination to live in loving harmony?

Jill P. Briscoe

⟡ A Place for Us ⟡

READ GENESIS 1:1–2:3.

In the beginning God created the heavens and the earth. . . . Then God saw everything that He had made, and indeed it was very good.
GENESIS 1:1, 31

*H*ospitality makes me feel loved. I grew up in a large family with more people than rooms, more tummies to fill than chairs at the table, and more company than you can imagine. Somehow my mother provided everything everyone needed. She stretched meals, created space, and served us well. She made places for people she loved.

I think of that when I read Genesis 1. God made a place for us. It was only going to be a few days before He crafted His most special creation of all . . . humankind, created in His own image. But first God, in His sovereignty, made a place for us: earth, a place of great beauty to enjoy and one that provided for our every need, and heaven, where we can live with Him forever. In the beginning He was preparing for us.

Mary Graham

✣ Poured Out Abundantly ✣

READ TITUS 3:1–7.

According to His mercy He saved us, through
the washing of regeneration and renewing of the
Holy Spirit, whom He poured out on us
abundantly through Jesus Christ our Savior,
that having been justified by His grace we should
become heirs according to the hope of eternal life.
TITUS 3:5–7

*G*race—God's unmerited favor—is ex-
tended to us from the Father, through
His Son, so that we can know and experience the power of the Holy Spirit to live a
new kind of life altogether. It is a supernatu-
ral life that is impossible to live apart from
the person of Christ and the control of the
Holy Spirit. Call it godly living—regeneration that produces a changed heart or justification—a freedom from sin and guilt.

People today are looking for that which
is "authentic." Nowhere is the "genuine"
needed to be seen and experienced more
than in the church and in the lives of those
who have received Christ as Savior. Are
you an authentic Christian?

Vonette Bright

❖ Living Freely ❖

READ GALATIANS 5:22–26.

*The fruit of the Spirit is love, joy, peace,
longsuffering, kindness, goodness, faithfulness,
gentleness, self-control. Against such there is no
law. And those who are Christ's have crucified
the flesh with its passions and desires.*
GALATIANS 5:22–24

*B*asically there are two kinds of diets:
the kind that restricts you to certain
foods in limited amounts and the kind that
says eat healthy, balanced meals in modera-
tion. On the first kind of diet, I'm always
hungry and cranky and feel deprived. On
the second, I feel healthy, in control, free to
eat what I want—and proud of myself when
I don't want to eat what I'm not supposed to.

Our spiritual life is similar. When we're
"plugged in to" our Power Source, our
character, personality traits, and values will
show it. That doesn't mean we'll become
sinless people. On occasion we'll still be
selfish, unkind, impatient, out of control,
or stressed out. But those will definitely
be the exceptions. Once plugged in to the
Power Source, we can live freely without a
set of restrictions. And that lifestyle frees
us to be all we want to be in Christ.

Dianna Booher

❧ Resting in Hope ❧

READ ACTS 2:25–28.

> *I foresaw the LORD always before*
> *my face, for He is at my right hand, that*
> *I may not be shaken. Therefore my heart*
> *rejoiced, and my tongue was glad; moreover*
> *my flesh also will rest in hope.*
> ACTS 2:25–26

While King David, the ancestor of Jesus, faced death and the grave, Jesus the Messiah met death and conquered it. Like a slave led in chains on our behalf, He willingly faced what, for any person, would have been the sure prison of death. But His body could not be separated from His Spirit like a mere man's. Sent to earth as a priceless vessel, He carried in His being the hope for humankind. In one brilliant stroke, Christ defeated the prince of death. The Conquering Hero then returned to declare to us the good news: *follow Me and live forever.* That is salvation.

Patricia Hickman

❖ Hearts Refreshed ❖

READ VERSES 4–7 OF PHILEMON.

*We have great joy and consolation
in your love, because the hearts of the
saints have been refreshed by you.*
PHILEMON V. 7

*J*oy catches us off guard. It is a response that wells up in our hearts from love. We can't control it, and we can't bring it about. We don't find joy; it finds us, often surprising us when it arrives, making us smile for no apparent reason, break into a tune when no one is around to hear it, or trust peacefully when things are falling down around our ears. Joy is never tied to wealth or circumstances or conditions, only love. A person who has every material possession might never experience joy, while someone who has nothing the world considers valuable may have joy like a rushing river. If you know love, you'll be surprised by joy.

Nicole Johnson

⊱ The Just Shall Live ⊰

READ ROMANS 1:16–17.

I am not ashamed of the gospel of Christ, for it is the power of God to salvation for everyone who believes. . . . For in it the righteousness of God is revealed from faith to faith; as it is written, "The just shall live by faith."
ROMANS 1:16–17

Simon wanted to know how to follow Jesus. "Simon, don't you know if you choose to follow Christ it could cost you everything; it could even cost you your life?"

Simon replied, "What does it matter anyway? I have nothing else to live for. Jesus is the only One who satisfies."

Simon was not ashamed of Christ and His gospel, even though he could have been killed for his newly discovered faith.

Let us follow the example of Simon and others who, at great expense to themselves, have chosen to walk by faith and not by sight.

Heather Mercer

⁕ Lavish Devotion ⁕

READ 1 JOHN 3:1–3.

Behold what manner of love the Father
has bestowed on us, that we should
be called children of God!
1 JOHN 3:1

John reminds the believers of the lavishness of God's love that is theirs—a love their opponents know nothing about! Apart from such grace and love there would be no "children of God."

God loves the unloved and the unlovely. He loves us when we hate Him. He loves us when we ignore or are indifferent to Him. That's what the love of God is like. It is primarily concerned with the others' well-being despite negative reaction or response.

"Like Father, like son," they say. The children should take after the Father. Do we love others as we have been loved of God? Do we love the unlovely and lavish love on those who ignore us, hate us, and despise us? The Holy Spirit will scatter such love around our lives if only we will ask Him.

Jill P. Briscoe

⟶ Abundant Pardon ⟵

READ ISAIAH 55:6–7.

*Seek the LORD while He may be found, call
upon Him while He is near. Let the wicked
forsake his way, and the unrighteous man his
thoughts; let him return to the LORD, and
He will have mercy on him; and to our God,
for He will abundantly pardon.*
ISAIAH 55:6–7

J remember once when we were visiting
non-Christian friends for the week-
end and several of us stayed up late playing cards. Toward the end of the evening, I
made what I thought was a joke. My card-
playing partner did not think it was funny.
He stormed out of the room.

All night I fumed about that moment.
He owed me an apology, I figured. But God
clearly laid it on my heart that I was wrong.
The next morning I approached my friend
and apologized. "Forgive me," I said. "I should
not have made that comment." The result?
My friend and his wife went to church with
us that day for the first time, and a few weeks
later they gave their lives to Christ. I'll never
forget the message of my all-night wrestling
match with God: "I have forgiven you abundantly; you must do the same for others."

Karen Kingsbury

⊹ Words of Truth ⊹

READ ECCLESIASTES 12:9–13.

*Because the Preacher was wise, he still taught
the people knowledge; yes, he pondered and
sought out and set in order many proverbs. The
Preacher sought to find acceptable words; and
what was written was upright—words of truth.*
ECCLESIASTES 12:9–10

*E*veryone is exhorted, "Fear God and keep His commandments, for this is man's all" (Ecclesiastes 12:13). There will be a judging of human behavior one day, so we need to use our tragically transient time on this planet to know and obey God's Word, finding His plan for our lives. The sooner we do this, the better. Don't wait until you are old and past it.

If we live in the present with an eye to the future, we will not find ourselves chasing the wind. Rather, we will discover that God will keep us occupied with "the joy of his heart" (5:20). It's all true, says the "Preacher." There is a God in heaven who cares about the way we live our lives on earth. We should take his warnings to heart.

Jill P. Briscoe

⁕ Enlarge Your Territory ⁕

READ 1 CHRONICLES 4:9–10.

*Oh, that You would bless me indeed, and
enlarge my territory, that Your hand would
be with me, and that You would keep me
from evil, that I may not cause pain!*
1 CHRONICLES 4:10

As we read this brief prayer of Jabez,
it becomes clear that this was not a
man who longed to accumulate wealth for
himself. He was instead a humble man de-
siring an enlarged sphere of influence, that
he might be more productive in carrying
out the plans and purposes of the God in
his life.

Here was a man whose heart was right
toward his Maker and whose motive for
asking touched the heart of God. The
result? God granted him what he request-
ed. Perhaps we should ask for the motive
of Jabez before we ask for the blessing of
Jabez.

Lana Bateman

❖ The Price of Peace ❖

READ 2 CORINTHIANS 13:11.

Become complete. Be of good comfort, be of one mind, live in peace; and the God of love and peace will be with you.
2 CORINTHIANS 13:11

I'm an optimist by nature, but I've decided we will never see peace on earth until Jesus comes to reign as the Prince of Peace. But Paul wasn't thinking about global peace when he wrote to the Christians at Corinth. He was thinking about peace in the church and in the family.

As I read Richard J. Foster's *Celebration of Discipline*, I was struck by his comments on the corporate discipline of guidance. If a church needs to make a decision, if the elders will come together, hear the facts, and pray together, we can expect the Spirit of God to make His will known to each elder. The key to success is found in Paul's admonition: "Be of one mind." For a church or a family to live in peace, they must be in agreement. They must also be willing to place the will of God above selfish interests.

Peace is not made in documents but in the hearts of those who are attuned to the heart of God.

Angela Elwell Hunt

❧ Healer of Broken Hearts ❧

READ ISAIAH 53:4–6.

*Surely He has borne our griefs
and carried our sorrows; yet we
esteemed Him stricken, smitten by God,
and afflicted. But He was wounded for our
transgressions, He was bruised for our
iniquities; the chastisement for our peace was
upon Him, And by His stripes we are healed."*

ISAIAH 53:4–5

*D*esperate circumstances often require that desperate measures be taken. Incurable diseases have driven people to faraway places looking for remedies. Others have depleted their financial resources for expensive prescriptions, hoping to be cured of what ails them. Some have even risked their lives during a surgical procedure trying to prolong life or improve health.

Jesus is the solution to what may seem an impossible situation. Isaiah prophesied that Jesus is the Healer of broken hearts, bodies, and spirits. Now is the time to seek Him for the answer you need. Then obey Him. Your answer is just a prayer away.

Babbie Mason

✦ His Way Is Perfect ✦

READ 2 SAMUEL 22:29–34.

> *As for God, His way is perfect; the word
> of the LORD is proven; He is a shield to all
> who trust in Him. . . . God is my strength
> and power, and He makes my way perfect.*
> 2 SAMUEL 22:31, 33

A funny thing happens when we choose God's way over ours: our way becomes perfect—perfect in its purpose and perfect in its plans. No, we won't always escape the long nights or bad phone calls; we won't walk through life with only clean health reports and paid bills. But God will be a shield around us, protecting us from the pain of life, underlining the joy in all things. He is sovereign God over all, our strength and our power. What could be more perfect than that?

Karen Kingsbury

Notes

$\mathcal{N}$otes

Notes

Notes

Notes

Notes

Notes